Note to Parents

Children may encounter new and unfamiliar people in a variety of situations. Such experiences can be unsettling and a little scary. It's natural for children to feel frightened by them, but they needn't feel helpless. This book helps children to recognize potential danger—and to avert it.

You will find **Never Talk to Strangers** a valuable teaching tool if you read it with your child. The illustrations show children in familiar settings—at home, at the store, at the bus stop, at the playground—and each time, an unfamiliar character appears on the scene. By discussing the different situations in the book with your child, you can help him or her to make the important distinctions between people who are "safe" and people to avoid. You might also want to make the book more real by acting it out with your child. Role-playing is a good way to capture a child's interest and attention, and it will help you get across important concepts effectively.

You can supplement the ideas contained in this book—and help insure your child's safety—by remembering the following guidelines:

- Instruct your child to stay near you in busy places, such as parks, shopping malls, beaches.

- Teach your child about the neighborhood, and remind him or her to play only in familiar areas.

- Instruct your child not to answer the door at home unless you are with him or her.

- Tell your child never to accept a ride from someone he or she does not know.

- Talk about safety with your child in a positive, nonscary way. Learning safety rules is a way for children to gain self-confidence, and should not be a source of fear.

—The Editors

Never Talk to Strangers

A Book About Personal Safety

By Irma Joyce

Illustrated by
George Buckett

A GOLDEN BOOK • NEW YORK
Western Publishing Company, Inc., Racine, Wisconsin 53404

If you are hanging from a trapeze
And up sneaks a camel with bony knees,
Remember this rule, if you please—
Never talk to strangers.

If you are shopping in a store
And a spotted leopard leaps through the door,
Don't ask him what he's shopping for.
     Never talk to strangers.

If the doorbell rings and standing there
Is a grouchy, grumbling grizzly bear,
Don't open the door. Mom won't care.
Never talk to strangers.

If you are in the park for a walk
And out of a cloud parachutes a hawk,
Unless you know his name, don't talk.
Never talk to strangers.

If you are waiting for a bus
And behind you stands a rhinoceros,

Though he may shove and make a fuss,
Never talk to strangers.

If you are out for a mountain climb
And a coyote asks if you know the time,
Let him wait for a clock to chime.
    Never talk to strangers.

If you're mailing a letter to Aunt Lucille
And you see a car with a whale at the wheel,
Stay away from him and his automobile.
     Never talk to strangers.

If you are riding your bike at noon

And you see a bee with a bass bassoon,

Don't stop to ask the name of his tune.
Never talk to strangers.

If you are swimming in a pool
And a crocodile begins to drool,
Paddle away and repeat this rule—
Never talk to strangers.

But...if your father introduces you
To a roly-poly kangaroo,
Say politely, "How do you do?"
    That's not talking to strangers
    Because your family knows her.

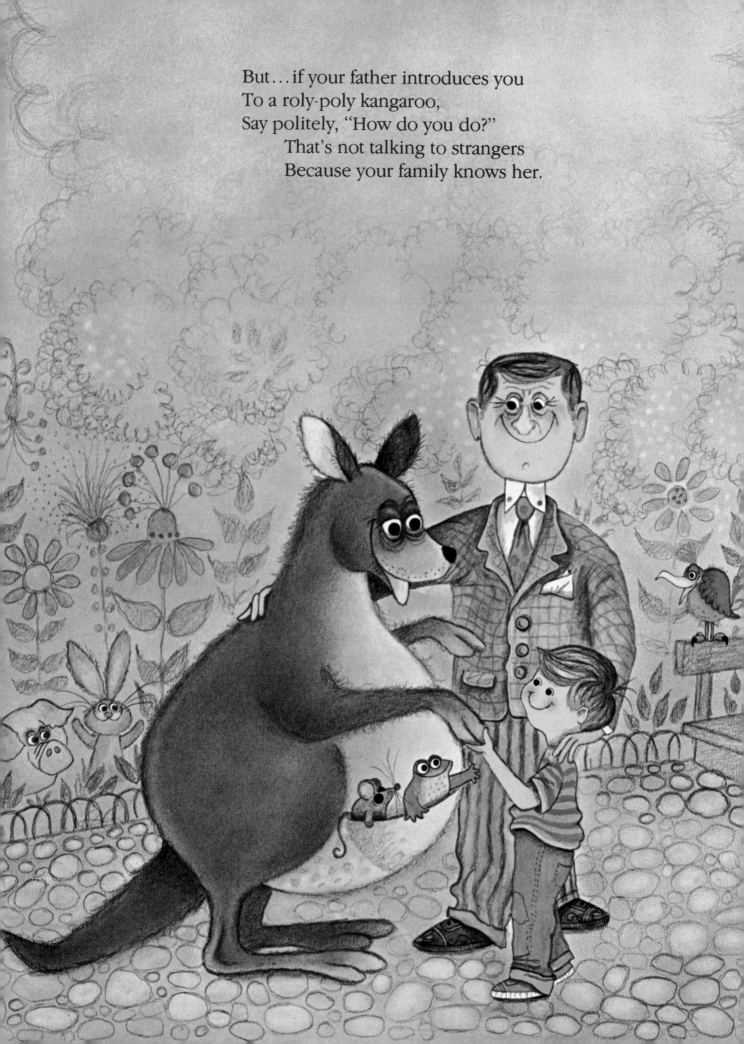

If your teacher says she'd like you to meet
A lilac llama who's very sweet,

Invite her over and serve a treat.
That's not talking to strangers
Because your teacher knows her.

If a pal of yours you've always known
Brings around a prancing roan,
Welcome him in a friendly tone.

That's not talking to strangers
Because your pal knows him.

If while eating toast and honey,
You see your friend the Easter Bunny,

Tell him a joke. He'll think it's funny.
That's not talking to strangers
Because he's *everyone's* friend.

Do you know why you've never heard
This jolly giraffe say a single word?
It's because she learned from a little bird—
Never talk to strangers!